To the
ZOO
Animal Poems

selected by

Lee Bennett Hopkins

illustrated by

John Wallner

Little, Brown and Company

Boston   Toronto   London

First Edition

Acknowledgments of permission to include previously published material appear on page 4.

Library of Congress Cataloging-in-Publication Data

To the zoo : animal poems / selected by Lee Bennett Hopkins; illustrated by John Wallner.
    p.   cm.
    Summary: A collection of poems about animals at the zoo, by poets including Myra Cohn Livingston, Theodore Roethke, and Maxine Kumin.
    ISBN 0-316-37273-0
    1. Zoo animals—Juvenile poetry.   2. Children's poetry, American.
[1. Zoo animals—Poetry.   2. American poetry—Collections.]
I. Hopkins, Lee Bennett.   II. Wallner, John C., ill.
PS595.Z66T6   1990
811.088′036—dc20   89-12559

Illustrations done in watercolor and colored pencil on Fabriano watercolor cold press paper

10 9 8 7 6 5 4 3 2 1

WOR

Published simultaneously in Canada
by Little, Brown & Company (Canada) Limited

Printed in the United States of America

For Nancy Larrick
for many years
— L.B.H.

For Tiggy, a zoo puppy
— J. W.

Acknowledgments

Every effort has been made to trace the ownership of all copyrighted material and to secure the necessary permissions to reprint these selections. In the event of any question arising as to the use of any material, the editor and publisher, while expressing regret for any inadvertent error, will be happy to make the necessary correction in future printings. Thanks are due to the following for permission to reprint the copyrighted materials listed below:

Donald J. Bissett for "Little Monkey." Used by permission of the author, who controls all rights.

Lee Blair for "Polar Bear" from *Hello, Pleasant Places!* (Garrard, 1972). Copyright © 1972 by Leland B. Jacobs. Used by permission of Leland B. Jacobs.

Gwendolyn Brooks for "Pete at the Zoo" from *Blacks*, published by The David Company, Chicago, Illinois.

Curtis Brown, Ltd., for "Camel" from *No One Writes Letters to a Snail* by Maxine Kumin. Copyright © 1962 by Maxine Kumin; "Seal at the Zoo" by Lee Bennett Hopkins. Copyright © 1972 by Lee Bennett Hopkins; "To the Zoo" by Lee Bennett Hopkins. Copyright © 1971 by Lee Bennett Hopkins. All reprinted by permission of Curtis Brown, Ltd.

Beatrice Schenk de Regniers for "If You Find a Little Feather" from *Something Special* by Beatrice Schenk de Regniers. Copyright © 1958, 1986 by Beatrice Schenk de Regniers. Reprinted by permission of the author.

Doubleday, Inc., for "The Hippo" from *The Collected Poems of Theodore Roethke*. Copyright © 1961 by Theodore Roethke. Reprinted by permission of Doubleday, a division of Bantam, Doubleday, Dell Publishing Group, Inc.

Macmillan, London, and Basingstoke for the excerpt from "Ostrich" from *Brownjohn's Beasts* by Alan Brownjohn.

Macmillan Publishing Company for "The Black Snake" from *8 A.M. Shadows* by Patricia Hubbell. Copyright © 1965 by Patricia Hubbell; "To a Giraffe" from *Catch Me a Wind* by Patricia Hubbell. Copyright © 1968 by Patricia Hubbell. Both reprinted by permission of Atheneum Publishers, an imprint of Macmillan Publishing Company.

Doug McReynolds for "Waiting at the St. Louis Zoo." Copyright © 1977 by Douglas J. McReynolds.

James B. Miller for "Here She Is" by Mary Britton Miller. Copyright by the Estate of Mary Britton Miller.

Putnam Publishing Group for "Supper for a Lion" from *All Together* by Dorothy Aldis. Copyright 1925–1928, 1934, 1939, 1952, copyright renewed 1953–1956, 1962, 1967 by Dorothy Aldis. Reprinted by permission of G. P. Putnam's Sons.

Prince Redcloud for "Of Wings." Used by permission of the author, who controls all rights.

Marian Reiner for "In This Jungle" and "At the Zoo" by Myra Cohn Livingston from *A Crazy Flight and Other Poems,* and from *Whispers and Other Poems.* Copyright © 1969, 1958 by Myra Cohn Livingston; "Zebra" from *Flashlight and Other Poems* by Judith Thurman. Copyright © 1976 by Judith Thurman. All rights reserved. All reprinted by permission of Marian Reiner for the authors.

Viking Penguin, Inc., for "Raccoon" from *Hosie's Zoo* by Leonard Baskin. Copyright © 1981 by Leonard Baskin. All rights reserved. Reprinted by permission of Viking Penguin, Inc.

Contents

Zebra

white sun
black
fire escape,

morning
grazing like a zebra
outside my window.

Judith Thurman

To the Zoo

I'm going to the zoo
    with you
       with you.

I'll try to stalk a lion
    and ride a kangaroo.

Then I'll climb a tall giraffe
    and laugh
And laugh and laugh
    and LAUGH!

When I've had enough of zoo
I'll leave it and go home
    with you
       with you
         with you.

Lee Bennett Hopkins

To a Giraffe

I'll get you a job, Giraffe!
Do you hear?
We shall build buildings together!
Marvelous buildings, Giraffe!
Skyscrapers!
I'll plan them for you alone, Giraffe,
The tallness of them,
The greatness!
Forget the lower floors, Giraffe,
We'll start them
Twenty stories high
And build from there.
Do you hear me, Giraffe?
Do you hear?

Patricia Hubbell

8

Camel

The camel's a mammal
who grouches and grumps.
I think that he wishes
he didn't have humps.

Maxine W. Kumin

10

Supper for a Lion

Savage lion in the zoo,
Walking by on padded feet,
To and fro and fro and to,
You seem to think it's time to eat.

Then how about a bowl of stew
With jello for dessert? Or would
A juicy bone be best for you?

Oh, please don't stare as though you knew
That I'd taste good!

Dorothy Aldis

11

Here She Is

Jungle necklaces are hung
Around her tiger throat
And on her tiger arms are slung
Bracelets black and brown;
She shows off when she lies down
All her tiger strength and grace,
You can see her tiger blaze
In her tiger eyes, her tiger face.

Mary Britton Miller

In This Jungle

In this jungle
I will search an elephant,
A huge elephant, gray, with pink eyes.

It is quiet now,
But I understand
That if I listen carefully,
If I crouch very still,
If I wait patiently,
He will come.

Boughs break.
Feet thunder
Branches fly.
And there will be a world of trumpeting

When he comes.
When my elephant comes.

Myra Cohn Livingston

14

Seal at the Zoo

I like to

    watch
    look at
    and see

The big, old, lazy
black-as-silk seal:

Hoping
that maybe just
one day,

I can

    touch
    and pet
    and feel.

Lee Bennett Hopkins

16

Polar Bear

Every time
I stand and stare
At the big
White polar bear,
I wonder
While he's
Swimming there,
If he has on
Long underwear.

Lee Blair

The Hippo

A Head or Tail — which does he lack?
I think his Forward's coming back!
He lives on Carrots, Leeks and Hay;
He starts to yawn — it takes All Day —

Some time I think I'll live that way.

Theodore Roethke

19

Little Monkey

Little monkey, soft and furry
Must you be in such a hurry?
Swinging high up in your tree
Come on down and talk to me.

Little monkey, soft and furry
Must you be in such a hurry?
I have no peanuts to give you today,
Won't you come down for a talk anyway?

Little monkey, soft and furry
Must you be in such a hurry?
Don't you want to be friends? Maybe not,
You don't even notice me — except when I've got
Peanuts to offer you. Is that fair?
Go ahead — play then, see if I care.

Little monkey, soft and furry
Please don't be in such a hurry.
Come on down from your place in the tree.
Come on down. Make friends with me.

Donald J. Bissett

Of Wings

Gazing
at birds
I sing songs
of wings.

Gazing
at sky
I, too,
want
to fly.

Prince Redcloud

22

From Ostrich

Little ostriches
fumble out of their eggs to be told,
'Patience is the thing, dear, an impatient
    ostrich
is making trouble for himself.'

An ostrich's life is a hard life which you
    sometimes
feel you could run away from.
Sometimes you even think it just won't
bear looking at any more.

But in the end it's a worthwhile
    job with good prospects and if you
        still want to apply to be an ostrich
        send for the forms today.

Alan Brownjohn

If You Find a Little Feather

If you find a little feather,
a little white feather,
a soft and tickly feather,
    it's for you.

A feather is a letter
from a bird,
and it says,
"Think of me.
Do not forget me.
Remember me always.
Remember me forever.
Or remember me
at least
until
the little feather
is
lost."

So . . .
    . . . if you find a little feather,
    a little white feather,
    a soft and tickly feather,
      it's for you.
      Pick it up
        and . . .
          put it in your pocket!

Beatrice Schenk de Regniers

24

The Black Snake

Black snake! Black snake!
Curling on the ground,
Rolled like a rubber tire,
Ribbed and round.
Black snake! Black snake!
Looped in a tree,
Limp as a licorice whip
Flung free.
Black snake! Black snake!
Curving down the lawn,
Glides like a wave
With its silver gone.
Black snake! Black snake!
Come and live with me!
I'll feed you and I'll pet you
And then I'll set you free.

Patricia Hubbell

Waiting at the St. Louis Zoo

After I'd bought balloons and
made monkey faces from picnic chairs;
after I'd scratched the walrus chin
and climbed the stairs
into the snake house and trembled past
the lion's lairs,
I always came back to the bears.

Doug McReynolds

29

Raccoon

The raccoon
       Steeped in starlight.

Tobia, Hosea, Lucretia, and Lisa Baskin

At the Zoo

I've been to the zoo
    where the thing that you do
    is watching the things
    that the animals do —

and watching
    the animals
    all watching
        you!

Myra Cohn Livingston

31

Pete at the Zoo

I wonder if the elephant
Is lonely in his stall
When all the boys and girls are gone
And there's no shout at all,
And there's no one to stamp before,
No one to note his might.
Does he hunch up, as I do,
Against the dark of night?

Gwendolyn Brooks